D0403046

**Put Beginning Readers on the Right Track with
ALL ABOARD READING™**

The All Aboard Reading series is especially designed for beginning readers. Written by noted authors and illustrated in full color, these are books that children really want to read—books to excite their imagination, expand their interests, make them laugh, and support their feelings. With fiction and nonfiction stories that are high interest and curriculum-related, All Aboard Reading books offer something for every young reader. And with four different reading levels, the All Aboard Reading series lets you choose which books are most appropriate for your children and their growing abilities.

Picture Readers
Picture Readers have super-simple texts, with many nouns appearing as rebus pictures. At the end of each book are 24 flash cards—on one side is a rebus picture; on the other side is the written-out word.

Station Stop 1
Station Stop 1 books are best for children who have just begun to read. Simple words and big type make these early reading experiences more comfortable. Picture clues help children to figure out the words on the page. Lots of repetition throughout the text helps children to predict the next word or phrase—an essential step in developing word recognition.

Station Stop 2
Station Stop 2 books are written specifically for children who are reading with help. Short sentences make it easier for early readers to understand what they are reading. Simple plots and simple dialogue help children with reading comprehension.

Station Stop 3
Station Stop 3 books are perfect for children who are reading alone. With longer text and harder words, these books appeal to children who have mastered basic reading skills. More complex stories captivate children who are ready for more challenging books.

More books by Ginjer L. Clarke

All Aboard Science Reader: Bug Out! The World's Creepiest, Crawliest Critters

All Aboard Science Reader: Freak Out! Animals Beyond Your Wildest Imagination

All Aboard Science Reader: Gross Out! Animals That Do Disgusting Things

All Aboard Science Reader: Fake Out! Animals That Play Tricks

For all of the dedicated, overworked
teachers and librarians, without whom our
children would be in the dark.—G.L.C.

To anyone who likes to sit and watch the
night.—P.M.

GROSSET & DUNLAP
Published by the Penguin Group
Penguin Group (USA) Inc., 375 Hudson Street, New York, New York 10014, USA
Penguin Group (Canada), 90 Eglinton Avenue East, Suite 700,
Toronto, Ontario M4P 2Y3, Canada
(a division of Pearson Penguin Canada Inc.)
Penguin Books Ltd., 80 Strand, London WC2R 0RL, England
Penguin Group Ireland, 25 St. Stephen's Green, Dublin 2, Ireland
(a division of Penguin Books Ltd.)
Penguin Group (Australia), 250 Camberwell Road, Camberwell, Victoria 3124, Australia
(a division of Pearson Australia Group Pty. Ltd.)
Penguin Books India Pvt. Ltd., 11 Community Centre, Panchsheel Park,
New Delhi—110 017, India
Penguin Group (NZ), 67 Apollo Drive, Rosedale, North Shore 0632, New Zealand
(a division of Pearson New Zealand Ltd.)
Penguin Books (South Africa) (Pty.) Ltd., 24 Sturdee Avenue,
Rosebank, Johannesburg 2196, South Africa
Penguin Books Ltd, Registered Offices:
80 Strand, London WC2R 0RL, England

Text copyright © 2008 by Ginjer L. Clarke. Illustrations copyright © 2008 by Pete Mueller. All
rights reserved. Published by Grosset & Dunlap, a division of Penguin Young Readers Group,
345 Hudson Street, New York, New York 10014. ALL ABOARD SCIENCE READER and
GROSSET & DUNLAP are trademarks of Penguin Group (USA) Inc. Printed in the U.S.A.

Library of Congress Cataloging-in-Publication Data

Clarke, Ginjer L.
Black out! : animals that live in the dark / by Ginjer L. Clarke ; illustrated by Pete Mueller.
p. cm.
ISBN 978-0-448-44824-4 (pbk.)
1. Nocturnal animals--Juvenile literature. I. Mueller, Pete, ill. II. Title.
QL755.5.C53 2008
591.5'18--dc22
2007042202

ISBN 978-0-448-44824-4   10 9 8 7 6 5 4 3 2 1

Black Out!

Animals That Live in the Dark

By Ginjer L. Clarke
Illustrated by Pete Mueller

Grosset & Dunlap

Do you ever wonder

what happens at night

while you are asleep?

When you are sleeping,

many animals are busy.

Some animals hunt at night.

They are called *nocturnal*.

Some animals live in the dark

almost all of the time.

Some creep in caves.

Some swim way down deep

at the bottom of the ocean.

And some cool creatures

hide out in dens underground.

Let's find out what it's like

to live in a black out!

Chapter 1

Animals Awake at Night

Is that a cat creeping in the dark?

No. It is a **genet** (say: je-NET).

This spotted African animal

looks and acts like a cat.

But it is related to a mongoose.

It hunts only at night.

This genet comes out of

its lair in a hollow tree

after the sun goes down.

It quickly climbs the tree.

Snatch!

The genet grabs a bird from

a nest with its sharp claws.

Another African animal hunts in the trees.

The **bush baby** has big, round eyes

that help it see in the dark.

Its name comes from the sound of its call.

It sounds like the cries of a human baby.

The bush baby can jump up to 20 feet!
Its long, fluffy tail helps with balance
so it can fly through the air.
This bush baby leaps in the trees
and pounces on a little lizard.

The **barn owl** lives in most
parts of the world.
It is a silent hunter,
and it has excellent hearing.
It twists its head around
to look for predators and
listen for faraway sounds.

Whoosh!

This barn owl swoops down quietly.

It catches a mouse with its talons.

Then it carries the mouse, in its beak,

back to its nest in a barn.

Some barn owls use nests that their

parents and grandparents used

before them.

The big, beautiful **luna moth**

lives only in North America.

It is one of the world's largest moths.

It has a wingspan up to six inches wide.

That's about as big as a bowl of soup!

This luna moth flutters in the dark

looking for another luna moth.

It is active only at night.

And it lives only for about one week.

It never gets to eat!

The luna moth does not have a mouth.

It lives only to make baby moths,

and then it dies.

But what a marvelous moth!

Big brown bats sleep during

the daytime.

They live in groups in

North American caves.

They also sleep in trees and buildings.

They are one of the largest bats,

with a wingspan of up to 14 inches.

That's about as long as your arm!

At night, hundreds of bats

fly out of a cave together.

They make high-pitched sounds

and then listen for echoes.

This tells them where their prey is.

This is called *echolocation*

(say: EH-ko-lo-KAY-shun).

The bats are listening for insects.

One bat can catch more than

one thousand insects in an hour!

Chapter 2

Animals in Caves

Many cave creatures are white.
It is so dark in the caves
where they live that they
do not need colors to blend in.
Some of them are missing
something else, too.
They do not have eyes!

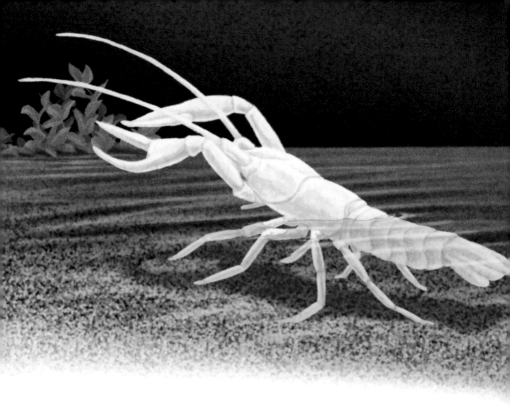

Cave crayfishes have probably
been around for millions of years.
But new types are now being found
when people explore new caves.
This crayfish uses its long antennae
to find its way in the dark water.
Snap!
It grabs food with its big front claws.

The **blind cave fish** has black dots
where its eyes should be.
It is totally blind.
Even though the blind cave fish
looks pink, it is not.
Its skin is clear, so that you can see
the blood vessels underneath.

Some scientists say the blind cave fish

is smarter than a dog!

It swims around things without

bumping into them.

And it seems to learn and remember

where things are in its cave.

Blind cave fish can even be kept

as pets in fish tanks.

The **blind salamander** is
white and eyeless.
It has feathery red gills
to help it breathe.
What a freaky-looking creature!

This blind salamander moves
its head from side to side.
It finds food by feeling for movement
in the water that tells it
something else is swimming nearby.
Chomp!
The salamander eats a tiny snail.

The **blind wolf spider** lives

only in the caves of Hawaii.

There are many kinds of cave spiders.

This one looks like a regular

brown and black wolf spider.

But it is only as big as a quarter—

much smaller than other wolf spiders.

And it does not have eyes!

This blind wolf spider does not
build a web like other spiders.
It hunts by feeling the ground.
Pounce!
It chases and grabs a tiny shrimplike
animal that is also blind.

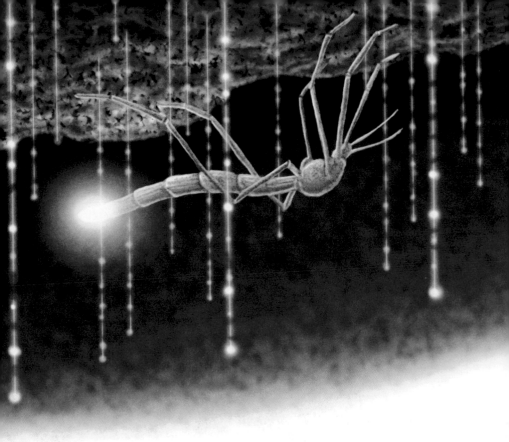

One weird cave creature

glows in the dark!

The **glowworm** is the larva

of a type of adult fly that lives

in the caves of New Zealand.

It uses small blue lights inside its body

to attract prey to its web.

This glowworm spins threads of silk

that hang from the cave ceiling.

Zap!

A moth flies into the silk strings.

The glowworm pulls it up and eats it.

When the glowworm is full,

it dims its night-light.

Chapter 3

Animals in the Deep Ocean

The **vampire squid** is more like

a jellyfish than a squid.

It gets its name because

its dark body and webbed arms

look a little like a vampire bat.

It also has big, creepy eyes.

This vampire squid sees a shark.

It flashes small lights on its head

to confuse the shark.

It wraps its arms over its body,

almost like turning inside out.

Poof!

The squid disappears into the dark.

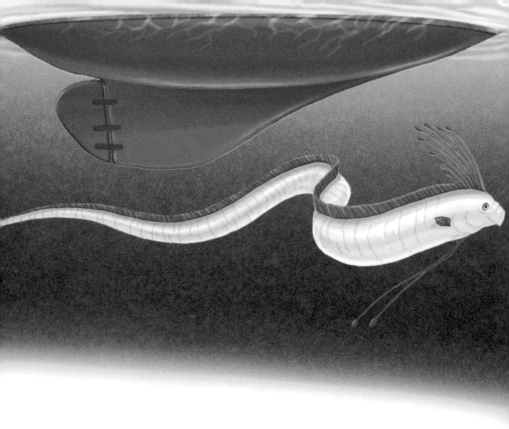

For many years, people have told
stories about sea serpents.
They could have been talking
about the **oarfish.**
Its very long body, spiky fins, and
bright red crest make it look like
a true monster of the deep.

The oarfish is the longest of all bony fish.

The oarfish can grow up to 30 feet long.

That's as long as some sailboats!

The oarfish is big, but it has

a small mouth and no teeth.

Slurp!

This oarfish sucks up a crab

and slinks away.

The **gulper eel** looks like a

huge mouth with a long tail.

It is also called the umbrella mouth.

It can eat fish larger than itself

by stretching its mouth to open wide.

The gulper eel wiggles its glowing tail.

A fish sees the light and

swims near the gulper eel's mouth

Gulp!

The gulper eel swallows the fish

in one big bite.

The **snipe eel** is long and skinny.

It looks like a piece of ribbon

floating in the water.

It can be up to five feet long.

But it weighs less than a chicken egg!

It has a thin beak like a bird.

The beak is full of tiny, spiky teeth.

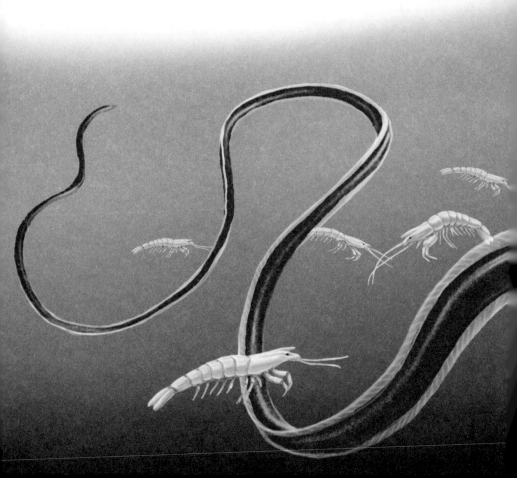

This snipe eel glides through the
dark water with its mouth open.
Swoosh! Swoosh!
It moves its head from side to side
to catch small shrimp with the teeth
in its beak.

Fish do not have legs.

But one fish can walk!

The **tripod fish** has three long fins
that it uses to stand on the seafloor.

The word *tripod* means "three legs."

This tripod fish stands still

on the ocean bottom.

It is waiting for food to swim by.

It uses its side fins like antennae

to sense movement in the water.

A snail bumps into the fish's fin.

The tripod fish grabs the snail

with its mouth and munches on it.

Chapter 4

Animals Underground

The **star-nosed mole** is almost blind.
It uses 22 feelers on its nose to feel
where it is going in the dark.
The star-nosed mole digs in
the ground like other moles.
But it can also swim and dive.
It eats worms, water bugs, and
even small fish and crabs.

This star-nosed mole finds a worm
in the dirt with its nose.
It picks up the worm with its feet,
stuffs the worm in its mouth,
and keeps on digging.

Most **badgers** live in family groups in underground dens during the daytime. The den has many rooms and tunnels. There is even a nursery for the babies. Badgers come out only at night.

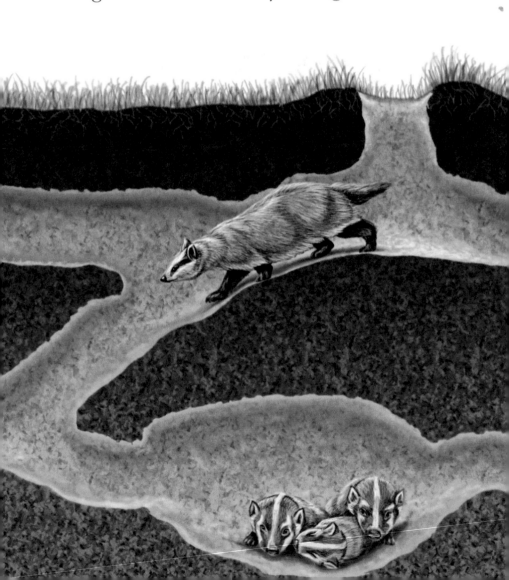

This badger sniffs the air for danger.

It comes out slowly to find food.

Scratch! Scratch!

The badger digs with its big front paws.

It smells in the dirt with its snout.

Badgers eat bugs, slugs, worms, frogs,

plants, fruits, and small mammals.

They are not picky eaters!

Prairie dogs make burrows

in the ground.

Many families share a burrow

and live close together.

Prairie dogs share jobs, too.

Some look for plants to eat.

Others take care of the babies.

They also take turns being lookout.

This prairie dog is guarding his

family's part of the burrow.

Another prairie dog comes close.

They crawl toward each other.

Smooch!

They know each other by their kisses.

If the prairie dogs do not know

each other, they will fight

until one runs away.

Bat-eared foxes live in dens. They usually hunt at night, and they have excellent hearing. These foxes have batlike ears that are much bigger than the ears of other kinds of foxes.

This bat-eared fox uses

its big ears to listen for insects.

It can hear bugs crawling in the dirt.

It especially likes to eat termites.

The fox scoops up some termites

and munches on them with its tiny teeth.

What a funny little fox!

Trapdoor spiders are sneaky hunters.

They dig deep holes in the ground.

Then they spin silk covers for the holes

and cover them with dirt.

These are called the trapdoors.

This female spider waits in her hole.

She lives in the same burrow

for all of her life.

Suddenly, she hears a noise outside.

Pop!

The spider jumps out of her hole
and surprises a cricket.
She grabs the cricket and quickly
disappears underground
to poison and eat the cricket.

Many types of ants live in huge
underground groups called colonies.
Honey ants dig deep colonies
full of lots of tunnels and rooms.
Like most ants, their colony has
one queen and thousands of workers.
The largest workers are called
honeypots.

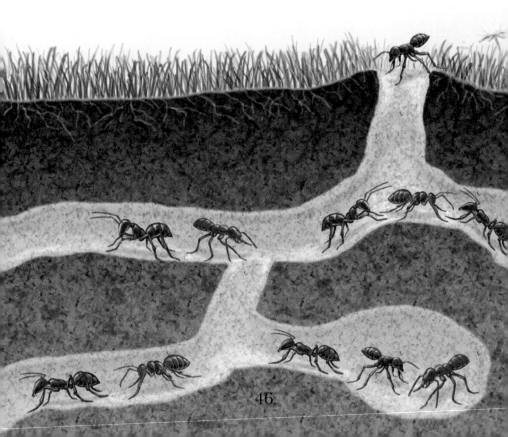

These honeypots hang in a cluster

from the ceiling of a tunnel.

Their bodies blow up like balloons

to hold the nectar they drink

from flowers.

The nectar is used to feed the queen,

who never leaves the colony.

Honeypots can be as big as grapes.

They get so swollen they cannot move!

The world seems quiet at night.

But many animals are awake,

hunting and hiding in the dark.

Hoo! Hoo!

Some of these creatures are noisy,

but they are just looking for food.

Good night, animals of the dark!